SURRENDERING TO WHO You Are

♥

ALSO BY THE AUTHOR

FREE YOUR SOUL - The Path to Greater Peace, Love, Joy, Health, and Harmony

THE HOME WITHIN - Haiku Poetry Prompts for Self-love Journal

LIFE ON FIRE JOURNAL - A daily prompt vision planner to thoughtfully plan, create your dream life, and fulfill your goals (pink, blue, and black color cover options)

Please scan the link above to view all the titles currently available by this author. Thank you.

**THE INSPIRATION TO CARVE A NEW PATH,
TAKE CHANCES, AND EMBRACE CHANGE**

SURRENDERING TO WHO You Are

♥

MURIEL OKUBO
DOCTOR OF ASIAN MEDICINE

Copyright @ 2024 by Muriel Okubo
Written and designed by Muriel Okubo
All Rights Reserved.

No part of this book may be reproduced, distributed, transmitted or amended in any form or by any means, including photocopying, recording, or other electronic or mechanical methods, without prior written permission of the publisher, except in the case of brief quotations embodied in reviews and specific other noncommercial uses permitted by copyright law. No graphics or images from this book may be copied or retransmitted without the Muriel Okubo's express written permission.

Hardcover ISBN: 978-1-998695-00-3
Paperback ISBN: 978-1-0688444-9-2
EBOOK iSBN: 978-1-998695-01-0

This book is dedicated to the love,
truth, and wisdom within us all.

Dear Friend,

Poetry is how my heart speaks.
It's simple yet powerful.
I love that I can share my soul
in a bundle of words.
I have loved the power of words
since I was a child.
They were my voice
when I couldn't speak
and sent in my letters
when we couldn't meet.
Words embody my thoughts
and the expression of my soul.
Sometimes, each letter holds
an emotion as I weep.
I let the words
express what's in my heart
and release them
beat by beat.
May they find a home
that lives and breathes
in your heart
as you embrace them too.
Thank you for being here.

TABLE OF CONTENTS

INTRODUCTION	1		BRILLIANCE	41
PERFECT MOMENT	5		CLIMB	42
REVERENCE TO THE PAST	6		ELECTROMAGNETIC	43
THE PAST	8		WHAT IF?	44
TAKE OFF	10		THE INGREDIENTS	45
FIRE	12		THREAD	46
NEWNESS	13		FEEDBACK	47
AWAKENING	14		TRUST	48
SURRENDER	15		ALIVE	49
INTUITION	16		RELEASE	50
ALL IN	17		INNER PEACE	51
PATHWAY	18		GLORY OF LOVE	52
REMINDERS	19		RIGHT TIME	53
CLARITY	20		BOTH PARTS	54
CHANGES	22		HEALTHY HOME	55
COHERENCE	24		OMIYAGE	56
BUILDING	25		KEEP ME AWAKE	57
RISK	26		JIGSAW	58
JENGA	28		HERE, THERE, EVERYWHERE	59
ONLY YOU	30		BEYOND	60
DISCOVERY	32		FOR YOUR GOOD	61
EVERY DAY	33		PURPOSE	62
POTENTIAL	34		GIVING GRACE	63
WARRIOR	36		DIVINE	64
BLESSED	38		EXPRESSED	65
ARISE	40		LAMP	66

WORKSHOP	67
THE WAY	68
ADAPT	69
POWER BOOST	70
EMPOWERED	71
UNLIMITED	72
LIVING ON THE EDGE	73
REVEALED	74
LISTEN	75
SAME MISSION	76
FOCUS	77
INFINITE	78
ON	79
PRESENCE	80
INSTANT	81
FLOWING	82
POSSIBLE	83
TUNED-IN	84
GUIDED	85
UNSTOPPABLE	86
SPROUTING	87
INGRAINED	88
INTEGRITY	89
BRIDGE	90
HIGHER	91
ON POINT	92
STICK-TO-ITIVENESS	93
KEEP GOING	94
FEED YOUR SOUL	95
WAVE	96
BETTER	97
ALL-SEASON	98
BOUNTIFUL	99
NEW LEVEL	100
ENERGY	101
DIVINE NATURE	102
UNLEASHED	103
FREE GIFTS	104
HARMONY	105
RIPPLES	106
CHOOSE WISELY	107
NOW	108
YOURS	109
ONE STEP AT A TIME	110
LISTENING	111
TRUST IN THE TRUTH	112
INVENTORY	113
NO END	114
WAKING DREAM	115
CAUSE AND EFFECT	116
PATIENCE	117
FAITH	118

INTRODUCTION

These poems are about surrendering to who you are—your inherent beauty, worthiness, and love. Life is an extraordinary journey with beauty, lessons, and challenges. Sometimes, it inspires and awakens you to carve a new path and take chances. Embrace the nudge.

Surrendering means living life, following your wisdom, pursuing your dreams, and saying yes to life. It's about finding a greater perspective of life and what it means to be alive. Embrace the transformation and let yourself bloom while enjoying every moment of the wonder of life.

The poems are also offered as a reminder of what change feels like when you are called to move to exciting places you've never been. The journey isn't always easy, but it's rewarding when you welcome every experience as inspiration to discover who you are.

Surrender to your gifts, talents, and what makes you feel free. Your treasures are revealed through exploration, openness, inspiration, and dedication.

When you connect with who you are, it'll feel like sunshine radiating from within. Bathe in it, bask in it, and be warmed by it.

Continue on your journey, allowing it to uncover the love you are—the true embodiment of the beautiful creation that is you.

You're a blessing, my friend.

PERFECT MOMENT

Sometimes we sit in silence,
waiting for spoken words of wisdom.
Sometimes they come.
Sometimes they don't.
When we can't hear,
we're being gently reminded
to let go
and surrender to the power we behold.
The wisdom we need is already here.

surrendering to who you are

REVERENCE TO THE PAST

With a bow,
you lay down the past—
you surrender your life,
your heart, yourself,
and release.
You arise
with a new life, a restored heart,
with you,
and with your truth.
You open your heart
to the heavenly skies.
You learned your courage, strength,
and survival in the past.
You learned your grace,
your fun, your joy,
and the softness in you.
In your wholeness,
you are.
The past has helped you
bring you back to you—
the truth of who you are.
You thank the past
with honour, respect, appreciation,

muriel okubo

admiration, acknowledgment,
and acceptance.
You love the past—
because of it,
you're free to be who you are.

surrendering to who you are

THE PAST

You created your identity in the past—
it was your saviour for a long time.
It feels stuffy now,
and you can't breathe.
You want to stretch your wings,
but the cage holds you in.
Your cage was thrown around a lot,
and everything felt sore.
You had to get out
because you had outgrown the past.
You open the door
you knew was there
but never gave regard
'till you reached your breaking point.
You're slightly disoriented
as you step out,
but you can finally breathe again.
You feel an excitement brewing within.
Your wings can open.
How far can they spread?
What is all this around you?
Do you remember a time when you weren't caged?

muriel okubo

Where do you go?
You sit down,
and the wind brings you new life.
Inspiration has come
and you take it all in,
because your spirit was meant to soar
and see new places.
This is what you were dying to be.

surrendering to who you are

TAKE OFF

If you keep one foot in and one foot out,
you'll never be able to fly.
You must go to the edge
and let the past fall away.
The past isn't where you're going—
but forward into the unknown.
It's so pretty yet unfamiliar
and your wings are a bit rusty.
You don't remember how to find your
balance.
You feel wobbly, and you fall a lot.
Every day, it seems to get better;
then, one day, your confidence will drop.
You don't think you can move forward,
because you remember
the cozy cage you lived in,
and it felt safe.
You sang your song all day,
and that was enough.
This new place,
you can't sing all day
or you'll be eaten alive.
As the sun hits your face
and the world is open to you,

muriel okubo

you know these new experiences
are part of leaving the past.
With a giant leap, you remember
those fears of the past
and the anchors that no longer hold you.
You were given your wings to fly.

FIRE

You almost died a few times in your life
and each time
you became more alive.
You learned that when life
gives you tribulations,
it's a setup for you to rise higher.
Each time, you never know
if you can get through it,
but you always know
it's not a place where you want to stop—
so you push yourself to keep going.
Each time, God ends up
turning all the rubble into wisdom,
and now you can see.
Shattering your limitations of the past,
you've learned to forgive more easily
because love releases you for more.
You're choosing to live,
because life shows you
how bright your light can be.

NEWNESS

This is new territory for you.
You love the freedom
and relying on your divine self.
There is nothing
you have desired more in your life.
You're not who you were,
and you enjoy who you are.
This is exciting yet vulnerable,
because the environment
has yet to catch up with you.
And when it does,
you'll be off on the next adventure.

surrendering to who you are

AWAKENING

You had to experience
a significant shift
in perspective,
that jolted you awake.
You can change your trajectory
in an instant,
or slowly over time.
Life is calling you to
unleash the beautiful vision
in your soul.
When you awaken to the truth,
you can use your imagination
to breathe life into places and spaces
that were sleeping
inside of you
and birth them into the world.

SURRENDER

You were pushed so far off the edge,
that you didn't know whether to scream
or to close your eyes.
You'd never been there before
and had never felt that way.
The only thing you could do
was open your wings and
pray they would support you.
You had to trust
you'd be given enough information
to direct your next steps
before you got there.
Sometimes,
you arrive before the information,
which gives you peace when it finally
catches up.
The gap is the hardest.
You allow yourself grace,
because you are teaching yourself
how to live again.

surrendering to who you are

INTUITION

You look at the past,
and it gives you fire.
You love all the painful things
that made you squirm, push, and scream.
You were too uncomfortable
to be caught in the stuckness.
Inside a cocoon,
it's dark,
and there isn't much room for movement—
it can feel suffocating at times.
This is when you push to explore the walls
to make space
and stretch what you know.
You're going to see what's beyond here
and what's beyond you.
Some people may say
it feels warm and cozy in a cocoon.
It's never been that way for you.
You know that if you stay,
it'll be the death of you.
You know this isn't your final destination,
and you won't be overstaying your welcome.
You want to see your wings open
and dance with the sun.

muriel okubo

ALL IN

You're taking a chance on yourself—
the most significant leap ever.
You don't know the future,
and you have no Plan B.
You're living each moment
with a sacred reverence.
You wake up with a purpose to live,
create, and let your heart be free.
You know what it's like not knowing
if you have another moment in front of you.
It's out of the ashes that you rise
and build a new fire.
You know that your heart will set this path
ablaze—
it's the divine truth behind all that you do.
You trust in it
with all your might
because, alas,
you're still here.
You'll let it lead you in all things,
for it has saved you in all the times before
when you thought its beat
was lost forever.

surrendering to who you are

PATHWAY

Every time we live from our soul's truth,
there are no mistakes or wrong turns.
Every moment is juicy and to be savoured.
The fire from our hearts
will burn strong with passion and purpose.
There are no regrets
when we're moved by faith,
and there's no need to relive the past.
We'll be full of stories and tales
of triumph, discovery, and freedom.
Be led by everything that inspires our soul.
This is our path set on fire.

REMINDERS

The past will always want to confront you
at times when you're ready to leave it.
That isn't a bad thing;
it's a perfect reminder
you had some loose ends to clear out.
In a fun sort of way,
it's here to show you
that you can deal with things
with so much more grace
than you thought was possible.
It can show you what you've overcome,
and further inspire your growth and passion.
You welcome every past thing
as you get better at facing
and releasing everything
that comes in front of you.
The past might skip the line
to meet you
and give you the gift of wisdom.
You'll take it and move forward.
Every
single
time.

surrendering to who you are

CLARITY

The past made us
want to fit in,
and now we don't want to fit in.
Sometimes, fitting in
is the worst thing we can do.
It trains us not to follow our heart's wisdom
or speak our truth.
It makes us invisible amongst
the background of the mundane.
To be who we are in this life,
we had to lose ourselves
to know who we are.
It's a bittersweet lesson
but a good one to embrace.
In many ways,
as we create our future,
we're learning the truth of who we are.
We're witnessing what gives us joy
and relinquishing what doesn't.
We've become aware
of when something feels manipulative
and, instead of second-guessing ourselves,
we choose to pay attention.

In waking up,
we understand there are traps everywhere.
Just because we live one way
doesn't mean the world lives the same way.
We can see it
now that we've become so changed.
And being ourselves,
we know it's okay to be different.
We're learning what it is
to belong to who we are.

surrendering to who you are

CHANGES

Take a chance on yourself—
what do you have to lose?
Sometimes,
the wisdom that arises
from being thrown into the fire,
will show you what you need to change.
When life hits you hard,
the impact will reset your vision.
You could continue to do what you knew
or you could venture into the unknown
and discover a whole new life.
You've dedicated your life to your purpose,
and with this life-changing experience,
you're ready to explore a different you.
It takes a lot of courage to leave something
that you know you're good at;
something that made you fit in,
something familiar.
You also know what it's like when
you almost die
and you come back to life
and you're changed—

seeking a part of you
that wants to be alive
and needs space to breathe.

surrendering to who you are

COHERENCE

Life will show us
when things aren't working.
Our heart desires harmony
with our mind,
and when it lacks it,
it feels dissonance and disconnect.
This is our cue that something
has to change.
With love and compassion,
we can discern what will bring us
back to coherence.
By surrendering to the truth,
we can move forward
for our best and highest good.

BUILDING

I'm not going to tell you it's easy,
because that's not the truth.
Even natural talent
takes time to develop
and for you to embody
the energy of a master.
Putting in the work
when you see no results,
and the mirror's image shows
you no favours.
Every bit counts,
fine-tuning your skills,
working through it again and again,
and spending countless hours
doing what feels like the same thing.
It's in repetition
that a knife gets sharpened,
that tears build muscles,
and each brick laid down builds a house.
Keep going when nothing
looks right,
because your vision
is leading to your sight.

RISK

We live on a rollercoaster,
never knowing when it ends.
Taking a risk and failing
isn't the worst thing in the world.
The worst might be
knowing we want to change
but let safety keep us the same.
Failures are what lead to success.
We all learn by failing,
making detours,
making mistakes.
Why wait another year?
Another month?
When will it ever be the right time
to follow the beat of our soul?
Our heart's wisdom will move us
in the direction we desire,
but we must choose.
Risk,
or risk maybe never.
Life is a big experiment,
and some people
never get the chance

muriel okubo

to surrender to who they are.
Life is right now.
Why not open your heart,
and allow goodness
to flow through it.

JENGA

What you do
may not be understood by many.
But you know precisely *why*
as you learn who you are.
Every pain that has come your way
was a blessing in disguise.
It helped you explore beyond
your comforts
and propelled you into the unknown.
The unknown is a beautiful place—
a space to create anything.
Everything you've ever experienced in life,
gave you the substance of who you are.
Like the bricks of a house,
it laid the foundation
for your adventures.
If you fall,
you can pick up the pieces
and rebuild from the rubble.
It's Jenga for life.
How many ways can you build a tower?
You're here to enjoy what's in front of you.
This is how you live a good life.

muriel okubo

Put your heart into your hands
and pour into the creation of your life.
Design it with love and gratitude,
and watch it come alive.

surrendering to who you are

ONLY YOU

When you step away
from the life you've built
and have known so well,
it feels uncomfortable to move
in a different direction.
You know the ups and downs
of your old life,
and venturing into new territory
brings new storms and challenges
you've never faced.
Seeing your old life
fade into the distance
can be scary,
but exploring new lands
and islands can also be exciting.
You can always learn,
so there is nothing to fear.
Life is a beautiful place
if you stay present to the beauty before you.
You're capable of creating art
in any way you please.
No one but you
knows what your soul

muriel okubo

needs from you—
which paintings still need to be painted,
which paintings are still unfolding,
which paintings are coming alive,
which paintings will be eye candy.

DISCOVERY

We all have things to learn
while we're here.
As we learn about ourselves,
we discover the gift of letting go
of things that don't fit
and receiving the things that do.
We're constantly evolving
and growing.
What works for us today
may not work tomorrow.
What worked for us yesterday
may not work for us today.
Let's be excited to discover
the richness of every day,
as we surrender to all that comes.
Life is constantly fine-tuning and
harmonizing us with everything
that is within.

muriel okubo

EVERY DAY

Carve a new path.
Make new tracks.
Be a light in the darkness.
Set ablaze a trail on new territory.
The cool thing is that life
is more exciting
when it comes from inspiration
versus the path of comfort.
Make whatever you do matter.
Give joy to the things that surround you.
Forgive the things that weigh you down.
Be happy for the things you encounter—
tough days,
better days,
happy days,
and every moment bridging them.

surrendering to who you are

POTENTIAL

Change is a curious thing—
sometimes, you crave it,
other times, you don't.
But life isn't meant to stay the same.
You're here to grow, evolve,
and be the best-fulfilled being
you can be.
Every path you take
has the potential
to allow you to do so.
Life's about not giving up
in the face of challenges
that will always come
as long as the sun rises.
But, rest assured,
the life force within you
can manage all of them.
Face the challenges as they come,
and you will transform them.
Don't look away,
because you have been blessed
with a shield of golden armour
that makes you resistant

to the things that aren't made
from the same ingredients as you.
You, my friend,
are protected.
So forge ahead.

surrendering to who you are

WARRIOR

Control is a funny thing.
We think we have control,
but we don't.
We think we have our lives
all figured out,
and then, in a flash,
it can change.
Life is unpredictable.
The only thing we can control
are our choices.
But the consequences,
we don't know.
It's the warrior
that can live in a world
knowing that we don't have the answers.
It's the warrior
that doesn't make the rules,
but learns to play without them.
There will always be those
who can't handle things
not going their way
and will manipulate others.
They are the weak ones,

taking juice from others,
leaving destruction in their path.
Be mindful that it's those who dance
under all circumstances
who are truly free.
Do the best you can
and let the rest go.
Be a warrior.

BLESSED

Unless it's necessary,
few people change.
We're servants to the past.
We do what we learn;
we repeat what we were told;
we're the reputation that precedes us.
In opening our hearts,
we find the courage to change.
Change takes deep spiritual work;
many would rather not
rock the boat.
In the pursuit of freedom,
change is a precursor.
There is comfort in the familiar,
but sometimes,
comfort is a prison.
When we are called to do different things,
it's our nudge to be open to more.
It's easier to close
in the face of challenge and tragedy
and to want to grasp more tightly.
But it's in the rubble
where we learn the beauty
of our humanity.

muriel okubo

We change to let ourselves grow
and break free
from self-inflicted limitations.
Space gives us the freedom
to move beyond what we know.
Our experiences allow us to share
more profound parts of ourselves
that have been cracked open.
Change seeps through all the open spaces
as energy seeks to express itself.
Change is vulnerable
but we would rather be free
than hold on to so much
that needs to be released.

ARISE

When we have a mission,
we can work endlessly.
We're creating something—
and living our vision.
We all need this—
something to wake up for
every
single
day.
Our sweat marks our creation.
There's beauty in strong hands.
There's strength in architecture.
There's flow in the mind.
There's dirt on our shoes.
There's another day of wisdom.
When we make it our heart's mission
to work from our soul,
the light will find its way.

muriel okubo

BRILLIANCE

Each of our challenges are different.
Perhaps challenges are put on our path
to keep our lives exciting.
Without challenge,
we would become soft and careless—
losing respect for each other.
No one has it easy.
We're meant to be tested,
tempered,
and shown our true strength.
We're made to endure
and reveal our beauty.
Diamonds are put under
extreme heat and pressure
and, somehow,
reveal more depth and radiance.
By overcoming our challenges,
we uncover
our unique beauty and brightness.

surrendering to who you are

CLIMB

You've fallen a million times,
but you know you can rise again.
Life gifts you with opportunity
after opportunity.
Each time,
you learn to climb higher mountains
and see with a greater understanding
and appreciation.
Every climb comes with challenges,
and you decide the worth
you'll milk from each one.

ELECTROMAGNETIC

The power lies in your heart and soul.
You know that you can do more good
through the fire in your heart
than from the bitterness of your tears.
Life is a constant choice
of where to put your focus and energy.
Let goodness flow through you,
animate all you do,
and be a magnet for the divine.

WHAT IF?

What if everything you deny here
or ignore here,
puts you back on Earth
to repeat the same lessons?
Surrender to the message you hear.

THE INGREDIENTS

Say yes to life.
Say yes to happiness.
Say yes to your call.
This is the recipe for surrender,
the recipe for all good things.

THREAD

Sweet soul,
you somehow came to read these words.
I think it's a miracle—
how my thoughts have somehow
reached your heart.
That's how I know this world
is full of beauty and grace.
Your spiritual eyes have made
my work meaningful and expansive
as you put your beautiful attention on it.
This is how I know that love
is the invisible thread connecting us all.

FEEDBACK

In surrendering to who you are,
you discover that inauthenticity
is not attractive to you.
It gives you dissonance
when someone's pretending,
or manipulating you.
You used to brush it off or doubt yourself,
but the truth is undeniable.
When you sense distrust in your body,
it's alerting you
there's a lack of integrity
in your presence.
You're free to walk away.
You're free to honour your intuition.
You can embrace and nurture this truth.
This is the coolest thing you've experienced.

TRUST

When we identify our needs
and embrace how important they are,
We move from a heart-led place
and are guided in the right direction.
Our souls know where it wants to go;
it just needs us to let go.

ALIVE

Use your life
to live the desires of your soul
and the desires of your soul
will come to life.

RELEASE

When we let go of everything
trying to break us,
we realize we've broken free.
We're no longer a reflection of the image
the past created for us.
We become a witness
to the way truth sees us.
With this divine power,
we rebuild and restore our temple
through the eyes of love.
With kindness,
we speak to ourselves,
with compassion,
we listen to ourselves,
with gentleness,
we nourish ourselves,
with patience,
we see ourselves,
with love,
we embrace ourselves.
We were made whole,
and now our reflection is the same,
looking in
and looking out.

muriel okubo

INNER PEACE

It's the same—
whether they know you
and don't like you
or they don't know you
and don't like you.
The conclusion is—
they aren't meant for you.
What an easy concept.
It's the same—
whether they know you
and love you
or whether they don't know you
and love you.
Love creates all openings,
ripe for possibilities.
Either way,
love wins.

surrendering to who you are

GLORY OF LOVE

Everything that broke you down
was a blessing to build you back up.
When you lose everything,
you get to start your life anew.
With clarity, you can envision
a different existence
and put your life back together
with intentionality and grace.
It's like piecing a puzzle together;
you must refocus on your vision
and see what fits and doesn't.
No more wasting time on things
that don't matter
or trying to make the wrong pieces fit.
Support what nourishes the plan
and cut away the things
that make you wither.
This is how you reconnect to your soul.
Permit yourself
to be the love of your life.

muriel okubo

RIGHT TIME

When we take a new path,
it's freeing and wild.
We allow our hearts to choose
and let the past settle in the dust.
We needed a new life,
so we created one.
There will never be a better time.
Sometimes discoveries happen
when we throw caution to the wind.
Our lives are now,
not when everything's perfect,
safe,
secure,
or trouble-free.
We all know how that turns out—
later,
soon,
never,
regret.
Everything good is right now,
asking us to move forward,
because chances like these
come only when we're inspired.

surrendering to who you are

BOTH PARTS

This life has shown you dysfunction,
cruelty,
selfishness,
greed,
hate,
but this life has also shown you beauty,
kindness,
altruism,
generosity,
and love.
When you can see
the beauty of this dichotomy,
you can make your next move—
your choice to choose love over fear.

HEALTHY HOME

The more we live life,
the more we understand ourselves.
It takes a lot
of being washed around
with the world's energy, ideas, and
disillusionment
to discover the wholeness in ourselves.
When we allow ourselves
to separate from all the chaos
and return to who we are,
we find peace
and acceptance
from the only place
where we needed it the most.

OMIYAGE

Everything that's come our way
has left us with a prominent gift.
One gifted us with sadness.
One gifted us with happiness.
One gifted us with anger.
One gifted us with kindness.
One gifted us with confusion.
One gifted us with peace.
One gifted us with weakness.
One gifted us with strength.
One gifted us with despair.
One gifted us with love.
After all these gifts,
let's be grateful
for everything we've received,
because now we can decide
what gifts to give back with our lives.

muriel okubo

KEEP ME AWAKE

I looked up
"spiritual awakening" in the dictionary.
It means to awaken
to the truth of who you are—
I will live with this
peace of being whole
over and over again
in the surrendering of me.

JIGSAW

No one has the answers except you.
We all have unique things to learn.
Sometimes, we wish the schooling
wasn't so painful,
or that it wouldn't take so long.
But, alas,
it can go
only at the speed
for which
we're ready.
And in reality,
we discover
there is no end to the learning.

muriel okubo

HERE, THERE, EVERYWHERE

The past gives us wisdom and truth.
The present gives us life.
The future gives us a promise.

BEYOND

We're all afraid of failing,
but if we don't try,
we can't realize our potential.
Staying the same,
we remain in the confines of safety.
In failing, we may feel pain,
but our capacity to grow
becomes larger,
and the field in which we play
becomes expanded.
Our spirit can soar
in its formlessness.

muriel okubo

FOR YOUR GOOD

Everything in life fits together like a puzzle.
Every step you took
led you to where you find yourself.
Everything you learned
can be used for your next project
or divine assignment.
None of it's been wasted.
Even your most significant failures
don't compare to your most outstanding achievements,
or the masterpieces waiting to be birthed.

PURPOSE

Challenge teaches us;
pressure will require us to
manage great energy.
When we use this energy
in meaningful, intentional ways,
it has the power to serve
and transform our lives.
With our energy—
who will we touch,
how will we use it,
what will we do with it,
when will we release it,
where will we focus it?
Our power lies in our energy.
As does our purpose.

muriel okubo

GIVING GRACE

The beauty of life
is that we accumulate
a lot of knowledge.
Through reflection and space,
we can see with clarity.
We each have much to share
with one another—
allowing us to
to bridge our challenges
with more grace.
This is the gift of life
that is for
giving.

DIVINE

When we have a cut or a wound,
a divine force within us
heals the skin
and returns it to peace.
When we utilize this force
with all our heart and soul,
endless miracles flow.

EXPRESSED

Life will come
regardless of what you're doing.
When you become more enlightened,
you can see from a greater perspective,
increasing the vision you have for yourself.
Every time you stretch,
there's a possibility for more greatness
to be shared, enjoyed, and experienced.
Use your life to your advantage,
and be as fully expressed
as you can be.

LAMP

The unknown can feel like a dark place—
a place of imaginary tales.
It can be the monster under the bed
or a fantastical place of treasure.
When confronted with uncertainty,
choose to bring your light to all things.
In this way,
it doesn't matter what you face;
your light will make it beautiful
because you're the one witnessing it.
Your light is what makes life bright
and boundless.
Shine more,
my friend.

WORKSHOP

We don't become experts
in anything
overnight.
It's the toiling, tinkering, and sweat
that makes us good at what we do.
It's the day-in
and day-out
as we continue to show up,
put our whole heart into it,
and give our best.
This is how experts are made
and not born.

THE WAY

The truth is
that some days
will be more challenging
than others,
and you'll question if you can make it.
Put one foot in front of the other
in the direction of your goals.
Be intentional with each step
and you won't fail
to uncover your destiny.

ADAPT

As you adjust to your new life,
things will become more manageable.
You'll get better at facing days
with more optimism and strength.
The things that used to cause you grief
will become less and less.
Moments of joy will increase,
as you learn the hoops.
Somehow, you're making your way,
and it's beautiful exactly as it is.
Day by day, you are creating your new life—
adjusting and adapting.

surrendering to who you are

POWER BOOST

Shake-ups have a purpose
in our lives.
They can shake us to move
in a new direction,
shake us to put more energy
into what we're doing,
or shake us into fright.
I choose to see shake-ups
as a realignment to who we are.
We're given a chance
to let go of loose debris,
solidify our structure,
and give us more fire
to live more passionately
with the life we've been given.

muriel okubo

EMPOWERED

Every lesson
comes at its perfect time.
We've lost good things
because of our lack of consciousness
in crucial moments.
In the willingness to be schooled,
we learn to take responsibility
for our actions.
This is a life
where everything matters
and, with this knowledge,
let's pray for a greater consciousness
to lead us to experiences
that are more like gifts
than grief.

UNLIMITED

When you do things from your soul,
a leap of faith is okay.
Your soul is vast,
and your life is infinite.
Be willing to explore your depths
to see how much you can sparkle.
Isn't that why you're here?

LIVING ON THE EDGE

Challenges can take you
to the edges of your life.
They can push you to release
the most authentic parts of you.
They can reveal where you're not living fully
and where you might venture
to give more love and energy
from the passion in your heart.
Embrace the silver lining of allowing
discomfort to free you.

REVEALED

Take some time to be with yourself,
to know who you are.
It doesn't mean you'll know everything,
but it'll give you a chance to listen
to the wisdom of your heart,
and the counsel of your soul.
This is the most sacred part
of your journey—
to be true to who you are;
the wholesome, loving being you are,
precisely as your creator designed you.

LISTEN

Taking a chance
at something that nourishes our hearts,
is never a bad thing.
When we deny our heart's desires,
we create dissonance within ourselves.
Our heart's wisdom will still knock,
but our lack of awareness will extinguish it.
This life is ours
to embody our wholeness.
The love in our hearts
will always continue to speak to us;
and the more we listen,
the better we'll hear.
Even our failures
will open us up to more possibilities.
What wisdom is calling on your heart?

surrendering to who you are

SAME MISSION

There are times when
things don't go
the way you want them to.
You'll discover the things
you thought were lost
aren't losses.
They weren't the right fit.
It didn't work,
because something was missing.
You can't expect a Michelin meal
without the right ingredients.
Instead of criticizing yourself,
understand that what you long for
is growing its way to you—
the heart that is wholly invested,
the breathable fit
where everything is present and ready.
Make your masterpiece
with the best ingredients
and with others willing
to make it so
with you.

muriel okubo

FOCUS

While attempting new things,
we'll learn perfection
rarely comes from the get-go.
It takes being a student
to become a master.
Don't expect it all to come easily.
We all have natural gifts and talents
but, without focus and intention,
rarely will we succeed.
Let our focus be led
by divine inspiration,
breath by breath,
and love will align us.

INFINITE

You are an unlimited being.
There are no limits
for the limitless.
Do your best with your whole heart,
and chances are
you will have lived fully.

ON

This world we live in
can get dark.
When we explore humanity,
we find great harm.
We all have a choice
of how we will be in this life.
We each have a unique blazing light
to be harnessed and directed
to supersede the world
with our illumination.

PRESENCE

In becoming comfortable
with uncertainty,
we learn that our present focus
is all we have.
Much energy is wasted on worry,
when today is our opportunity.
Let the worry of tomorrow
come later.
For now,
let's focus on being free
in the only moment there is.

INSTANT

We don't need
everything figured out.
Sometimes,
the best gifts come
when we stop controlling our lives.
Inspiration drops in,
giving us light
where there was none before.
Light-bulb moments
fire our hearts and souls
and ignite a blaze forward.
This is the beauty of creation.

FLOWING

Surrendering—
it's allowing,
it's trusting,
it's letting go,
it's being receptive,
it's acknowledging what is,
and being open to what's beyond.
Surrendering
is magical,
when you're used to resistance,
pain, and suffering.
In surrendering,
you allow everything to move,
maintaining flow,
while opening you
to the beauty of the truth.

POSSIBLE

Your feelings toward
the outside world
are based on your perceptions.
And if you feel
you may be judged,
you probably will be.
If you change your perception,
the world changes too.
If you don't care that you'll be judged,
the energy stops there.
Apply energy to what matters.
The judgement of others
is less about you
and more about their limitations.
The power lies within you.
What are you capable of creating?

TUNED-IN

This world is made up of patterns.
Harmonious patterns
are all around us—
the spectrum of green in plants,
the flowering blooms,
the perfection of a water droplet,
the sound of a baby's laughter,
the crystal reflecting light,
the flicker of a flame,
the bee's creations.
Everyday,
beautiful processes such as these
are all symbiotically working together
like an orchestra.
The tuning of one,
allows the rest to find resonance.
This is what life is—
using love to tune us
to our inherent brilliance.

muriel okubo

GUIDED

Whatever path you choose
will have challenges.
The old path challenges you
to be the same
when your soul desires growth.
The new path challenges you
to grow
when you don't know how
to do it with grace.
The key to choosing
the right path
is to make a choice
based in love
and not fear.

UNSTOPPABLE

Sometimes,
when you love something,
it doesn't matter how hard things get,
you won't quit.
It's like the only thing
that keeps you afloat
when the heat's turned off,
and you have no food.
It's the dream
that wakes you every day
when the only signs of success
are invisible
visions in your head.

SPROUTING

It's your responsibility
to hold the vision for your life—
to nurture,
feed,
and care for it.
It's okay if the world doesn't see it
or appreciate it
in the way you do.
Your purpose is to honour your soul
and bring life to the things
that ignite it.
This is the wonder of a seed
that blossoms into beauty
where once only you may have believed.

surrendering to who you are

INGRAINED

Everything in your past
has been a blessing for your present.
Every struggle
taught you the gift of growth.
Every heartache
taught you the gift of true love.
Every loss
taught you the gift of appreciation.
Every failure
taught you the gift of another chance.
Every mistake
taught you the gift of perspective.
Every injustice
taught you the gift of honesty and fairness.
Every inequity
taught you the gift of choosing love
in the face of evil.
You are alive with the wisdom to know
that everything is laced with good,
and now embedded in you.

muriel okubo

INTEGRITY

If your choice
here on Earth is to grow,
you will be given
significant opportunities
in which to receive it.
If your soul
has things it wants you to do here,
it will trigger you to go deep
until you reach them.
The soul is working
its way through you
to find unity in who you are
and everything you embody.

surrendering to who you are

BRIDGE

Sometimes,
it's all the things
that crack and destroy
your sense of self
that frees falseness
and allows your true self
to emerge.
This is the soul's work
to bring you as close
to the truth as possible.
It wants you to merge
with the greater consciousness
of who you are
and surrender to the gift you are.

muriel okubo

HIGHER

Most of the good things in life
come from seeds planted long ago.
The gifts, talents and inspiration
you had as a child
is when heaven
spoke strongly through you.
Given space,
the truth will emerge.
When you see a giant tree
and marvel at its beauty,
you forget all the storms
and attacks it weathered
to be as resilient as it is today.
Cherish the experiences
that enlivened your dreams
as you release the treasures of your heart.
Take hold of the truth,
and move from your soul.
This blessing of growth
helps you reach new heights
as the sun reminds you which way to go.

ON POINT

There's often a lot of effort required
in carving a new path
or unleashing a passion
found deep within.
It's the persistence, diligence,
and patience
that keeps your fire burning
long after the darkness has settled in.
If it's on your heart,
there will be an invisible drive
that moves you
even when you see no progress.
Keep going,
dear one,
you're a fire
with goodness directing your flow.

STICK-TO-ITIVENESS

This life is yours.
No one is going to know
what's best for you—
except you.
When you follow your heart,
you place a bet on yourself.
Now it gets real,
and you appreciate the concept
of sink or swim.
When your heart is entirely in it,
you'll learn to swim
regardless of how tired you feel,
how choppy the waters are,
how stormy the sea,
and how many sharks swim about you.
If you stick with it,
you'll learn how to
motivate yourself,
calm yourself,
build a raft,
and keep moving despite all the threats.
Only when your heart's in it,
will you have given it your best shot.

surrendering to who you are

KEEP GOING

It isn't in the easy
that we grow,
or have success.
Most enduring successes
have taken years
of committed effort
and finding a way
through the roadblocks.
When things get hard,
know that everything new
will challenge us
and, in time,
grace will greet us
if we don't give up
on ourselves.

FEED YOUR SOUL

Follow the vision of your soul,
not the temporary whims of this world.
One gives everlasting peace,
and the other feeds a black hole.
Follow your divine light within,
and you'll discover
what feeds your soul endlessly
versus what leaves it
unquenchably drained.

WAVE

Change is inevitable.
You can try to resist it,
but the more you do,
the more you lose your flow.
If you deny that change will come,
it'll move past you,
or completely wash you away.
Let awareness be your friend.
Embrace change as your ally,
and it'll assist you.
Sometimes,
when a wave of change arrives,
you must catch it.
Good things are always coming,
and the good waves
are waiting to be ridden by you.
Go surfing, my friend,
and find your next wave.

muriel okubo

BETTER

When we leave Earth school,
may it have taught us
love,
humility,
perseverance,
patience,
kindness,
and gratefulness.
It's for a fleeting time
that we're here
to absorb these truths,
and may we leave it better
than when we came.

ALL-SEASON

In a world
full of roaming souls,
you are here,
to be your unique self.
Your soul is not lost;
it was planted here,
in this season,
for you to bloom and grow—
to be all you are.

muriel okubo

BOUNTIFUL

Surrendering to who you are
means doing what makes
your soul feel alive.
It's reconnecting with everything
that makes you, you.
In giving yourself the space
to recognize the gifts you have,
and cultivate what remains
untapped within you as you evolve.
Through accepting your wholeness,
you can unleash the treasures
you hold within.

NEW LEVEL

When life changes,
embrace the transformation.
It's in the flow
that you find harmony
within and outside of yourself.
When you stop resisting
the call to change,
you allow your natural rhythm
to be unleashed.
Use all change
as a reminder
that this season
is giving you extra grace
to move, jump, and be propelled
to higher perspectives
and higher places.

ENERGY

Life will show us exactly
what we need
to grow.
It'll call out to us
signalling distress
or excitement.
This is our opportunity to listen
and be willing to hear.
Distress will instruct us
to become a student,
and excitement will direct us
to become a master.
By harnessing our energy,
we can determine
how we want to move.
Becoming a student,
we're reminded of all we do not know
and, as a master,
we're reminded to remember what we do.
The beauty of this life
is that we have the grace
to be both.

DIVINE NATURE

Unfold with life.
Resistance won't help you avoid
what you don't like.
By acknowledging what is,
you allow the unnecessary
to flow past you,
while enabling you to change
what you can.
By embracing all that comes,
stay in harmony with your being.
Default to your divine nature,
and all of life will
shape to support you.

UNLEASHED

When you make intentional changes
because you want to make things
better for yourself,
you'll find, at first,
that it'll challenge you.
Surrender to the discomfort,
feel the resistance,
and keep going.
When things get hard,
it isn't a sign to give up.
Almost all meaningful things
will be hard.
If your heart's in it,
there is magic to be released.
Choose hard,
and focus your fire
on where it's being called.
Keep fanning the flames,
and the fire will grow.
If you don't give up,
your heart and soul
will reveal the blessings
that are living within.

surrendering to who you are

FREE GIFTS

Divine love, wisdom, grace,
peace, intelligence—
are available to you
when you surrender to your wholeness.
It's your nature to flow abundantly
with all this beauty.
Allow these divine gifts to circulate
freely in your life.
They'll guide you on your path,
bringing perfect opportunities
and wonderful blessings
of goodness and cheer.

HARMONY

When you're good at something,
it's because every day
you chose to focus on doing the tasks
that called to your soul.
You become a finely tuned instrument—
a handpiece of God.

RIPPLES

Sometimes, you want to make change
transpire more quickly than it's happening.
In these times,
allow yourself to appreciate
everything you've done
to move the needle in the direction
of your desires.
Celebrate yourself,
breathe,
and remember,
that positive energy is rippling
everywhere,
with all you've done already,
and even when you let go.

CHOOSE WISELY

When you experience discomfort,
it's the unconscious mind in operation.
When you experience inspiration,
it's the divine creator operating through you.
One lies to you—
telling you
you're not enough,
and the other tells you the truth
to free you.
Choose to soar
when you discover
that you have the choice
of which one
you'll give your attention to.

NOW

No one knows what tomorrow,
or even the next moment holds.
Put your heart into what makes you
alive with life,
infused with love,
swallowed in creation,
swimming in your spirit.
Freedom in this moment
is your sole source of bliss.

muriel okubo

YOURS

This moment is yours.
When you close your eyes at night,
you're the same person
doing this since you were a baby.
Choose to rest in the good you've done
and rise with the good you'll do.
Live intentionally,
infusing your life with meaning.
Give it direction,
release its power,
and move with purpose.
Let love be your backdrop
and truth your source.
Surrender yourself,
and let your beauty unfold.

ONE STEP AT A TIME

The more time we spend resisting life,
the more energy we invest
in keeping ourselves distanced
from our freedom and joy.
Recognizing this,
we can be open
to what needs tweaking,
what needs repair,
what needs a shift,
or what needs an overhaul.
Do the things that call to you,
one step at a time.
More gains can be made with one step,
than nothing at all.

LISTENING

That creaky stair,
that broken lightbulb,
that muddy floor,
that damaged roof—
problems don't go away when we ignore them.
Chances are the issues become worse
if they stay unaddressed.
Our discomforts enter our awareness
because they cry out to be heard.
Most cries are indicative of pain—
areas calling for change and movement.
All we can do is manage what we can
when something calls our attention.
A little hammering,
a little change,
a little clean-up,
a little patch.
All these little things,
will free us to keep moving;
strong, agile and flexible,
on our path.

TRUST IN TRUTH

When you surrender,
it has nothing to do with weakness
nor admission of failure,
but rather a gift of grace.
By surrendering to who you are,
you release your strength,
your knowingness that you're loved,
and that you're here for a purpose.
In surrendering,
you create a space to appreciate
everything you are
and allow yourself to trust
in the beauty of who you are.
Surrendering is opening
and giving yourself permission
to be powerful.

muriel okubo

INVENTORY

Suddenly,
when you are confronted
with a lack of time,
devastation, injury, illness, or death,
everything in life takes a new perspective.
You'll wish you had more time
to be doing this or that.
Everything that wasn't important
suddenly becomes important.
Everything that was important
suddenly loses its priority.
Let your life
show you how you want to *live* more,
what your needs are,
what your wants are.
What brings out the best of who you are?
Don't wait for the stealers of life
to remind you
of the light you are.

surrendering to who you are

NO END

Who you are
is not defined
by other people,
by your job,
by how much money you make.
It's defined by what makes you
you light up,
feel joy,
feel fire despite the challenge,
rise when others want to sleep,
wake with energy.
This is who you are—
a love that knows no end.

WAKING DREAM

It's in your childhood
that you were the closest to knowing
what made your soul feel free.
Before anyone told you
what you needed to do
to conform to this world,
what made your soul feel free?

CAUSE AND EFFECT

We become stronger
because we've been put through fire.
We become wiser
because we've lived through harsh times.
We become more prosperous
because we've gained wealth through loss.
We become more ourselves
because we've made friends
with our worthiness.
Indeed, this life is one of grace.

PATIENCE

Change will challenge you
especially when you're trying
to integrate yourself
and everything in your world.
Often, you'll get pulled
in different directions,
as you try to make your life congruent
to who you are.
This is the nature of change;
it moves everything.
Be sure to remind yourself gently
that not everything must happen
right away.
Be patient and kind to yourself;
and find joy and peace in the process.
It's coming together…

surrendering to who you are

FAITH

We all have a comfort zone
of what security looks like.
In taking chances,
we often learn about discomfort
and pain points.
We learn we're more durable
than we give ourselves credit for.
Only when we take a chance on ourselves,
will we know if the risk was worth it.
Unless we test ourselves,
how else will we know
what we're capable of?
Life will show us repeatedly
that we can overcome much more
than we perceive.

You are still here, my friend—
stronger,
smarter,
wiser,
than ever before.

muriel okubo

Every good thing
came from getting past our perception.
We must decide
what our next adventure holds,
and give it our all
until we uncover the truth of our soul,
even when we feel uncomfortable
or incapable.

My friend,
choose your greatness—
all that waits to be revealed
just beyond what your eyes can fully see.
This is faith.

THANK YOU FOR PURCHASING 'SURRENDERING TO WHO YOU ARE'

Sharing my writings from my heart is one way that my soul speaks. Every book I write comes from a sacred place of love and joy. I pray that the messages prosper the hearts and minds of everyone who reads them. I am so happy my book made its way to you.

If you've found 'Surrendering To Who You Are' to be a source of inspiration and value, I'd love for you to share your thoughts in a review. Your feedback is greatly appreciated. Thank you once again!

Warmly,

Muriel Okubo

SUBSCRIBE TO MY NEWSLETTER

Find me on my website: okubowellness.com
Follow me on IG: @muriel.okubo & @okubowellness

ABOUT THE AUTHOR

Muriel Okubo is a Canadian-Japanese author, artist, and Doctor of Traditional Asian Medicine. She has had a busy practice for over sixteen years in which she has treated people from all walks of life and all ages struggling with various issues. Having witnessed the pains of the human condition and the beauty of the human spirit, she wishes to inspire and encourage everyone on their path.

Understanding that body-mind-spirit health is crucial for wellness, she has created beautiful books to help people integrate their physical, mental, emotional, and spiritual bodies. She has always loved the power of writing as a connection to her heart and soul. Muriel is passionate about sharing the ideas and practices that have helped her the most on her path to living more consciously. She desires that everyone follow their inner wisdom and find the truth of their soul.

www.ingramcontent.com/pod-product-compliance
Lightning Source LLC
Chambersburg PA
CBHW030443010526
44118CB00011B/770